CHICHESTER 10

PORTRAIT OF A DECADE

Chichester 10

PORTRAIT OF A DECADE

BY ZSUZSI ROBOZ

WITH WORDS BY STAN GÉBLER DAVIES

DAVIS-POYNTER

LONDON

FIRST PUBLISHED IN 1975 BY DAVIS-POYNTER LIMITED
20 GARRICK STREET LONDON WC2E 9BJ

ISBN 0 7067 0161 5 (cased edition)
ISBN 0 7067 0194 1 (paperback edition)

Designed by Malcolm Young MSIA MSTD

Filmset and printed in Great Britain by
BAS Printers Limited, Wallop, Hampshire

Contents

To Teddy my husband, for everything

Introduction

BY SIR JOHN ROTHENSTEIN

When Sickert wrote 'Taste is the death of a painter; the more art is serious the more it will avoid the drawing rooms—stick to the kitchen' and the like, he was expressing a preference shared by many artists today for the extraction of beauty from subjects drab or even ugly in themselves, to depicting subjects of obvious beauty or distinction.

Sunsets, sunrises, moonlit landscapes, men and women of obvious beauty and distinction are subjects that artists rarely undertake except from necessity. Portraits of such people are of course, constantly commissioned, but often, I believe, carried out with a degree of reluctance. Everything, they are inclined to feel, that can be said of subjects of obvious beauty, after many centuries, has already been said.

There are, however, exceptions. Among them is Zsuzsi Roboz; she is not, I believe, under economic necessity to make portrait drawings of people of obvious beauty and distinction. She does so for preference, depicting these qualities for the sheer pleasure of it, yet—at least in the case of the subjects known to me—without a shadow of flattery. It is rather that she takes faces not only as enjoyable in themselves, but as media for the acute perception of the character which they may either express or conceal. To portray the conspicuously attractive face searchingly is not as natural as it was, say, in the time of Gainsborough or even Watts. At a time, therefore, when such portraiture, as indeed portraiture in general, thanks to the invention of the camera and a variety of other circumstances, has become a particularly exacting art, the best of Zsuzsi Roboz's portrait drawings are exceptional achievements.

JOHN ROTHENSTEIN

Sir Alec Guinness

Sir Alec knew Eliot, in fact created his part in the original production of 1949. 'I just think good writers are simply marvellous. I am very snobby about having known people like T. S. Eliot and Graham Greene. I mean, if a Duke said "drop in" I wouldn't bother, but if Graham Greene said so I'd rattle around in a flash. I would like to belong to that sort of circle.'

Sir Alec's belief in Eliot was vindicated. The revival of this 'difficult play' travelled to London. Sir Alec was Riley, a character somewhat modelled on Freud, Eileen Atkins his leading lady. Asked a little while later about up-and-coming actors, he said 'Among the girls, Eileen Atkins is in a class by herself.'

His reputation as a perfectionist is not without foundation, and yet he says he might have been happier being less painstaking. He discovered a saying of Chesterton's—'What's worth doing is worth doing badly'—and says he wishes he had found it years before. 'What's worth doing is worth doing.'

Other Guinnessisms: 'If someone offered me £100,000 tomorrow I would never act again.' 'I often think that I was intended to be a small-part actor.' 'I calculate that if the ten of us in this country who make the most from film contracts pooled our tax, it would not only have built the National Theatre but run it for several years.' 'I am the repository of very odd bits of information.' 'I have not only a sense of the past, but a sense of the little oddities of the past.'

What else does one say about Alec Guinness without writing a book about him?

Billie Whitelaw

Billie is called Billie because her father got a little absent-minded after leaving the house to fill out her birth certificate, became confused and forgot to register her as Diana. During the early part of her career she played boys on the radio. Sophia Loren had similar trouble establishing her identity as a female. Both ladies seem to have recovered quite nicely from the disability.

Miss Whitelaw used to be regarded as an actress who was most appropriate to working-class drama, made the pilgrimage to Stratford East for £12 a week and agonized in the *Daily Worker* about the H-Bomb and other bothersome topics. She also appeared in many memorable films, then decided the bottom of the kitchen sink had been more or less scraped bare and turned her attention to the classics.

Such, almost, is *The Dutch Courtesan*, a ribald black comedy by John Marston, Shakespeare's junior, who got into bad trouble for poking fun at the wrong people and ended his days, appropriately for a satirist, as a country vicar. Miss Whitelaw played the name part, which calls for, and got, a good deal of extravagant sex appeal and the sweet enunciation of foul language.

'I think we have it in us to be nuns and prostitutes,' she has said. 'Every woman is all things in between.'

Miss Whitelaw did not have drama training and does not pretend to understand all the parts she plays, which does not prevent her from collecting awards with monotonous regularity, or Samuel Beckett from putting her in his plays. (He coached her for *Play* at the Royal Court.)

'I've been in two Beckett plays and I didn't know what was going on at all. I'm what you might call an instinctive actress, not one of your deep thinkers. There's nothing much upstairs in my think-box. But you get this feeling that something is right and true and you go ahead.'

Robon

Sir John Gielgud

Sir John says he was offered the part of Caesar in the film production but turned it down out of dislike for Gabriel Pascal, the wily Hungarian who turned up penniless on Shaw's doorstep and talked him into giving him the rights to film his works. He is inclined to attribute his success in Roman parts to the advantage of having a large nose.

'Shaw asked me to play Caesar in the film with Vivien Leigh, but I turned it down. It was silly of me. Claud Rains played it and made all that money. Also I would have got to know her sooner. I did not meet her until much later.'

Gielgud as Caesar advanced onto the open stage, which he admits he initially found quite frightening, and addressed his marvellous opening speech (the inspiration pinched by Shaw from Napoleon, incidentally) not to the Sphinx but directly to the audience. It was a strange opening (not so strange, perhaps, given the bizarre form the Sphinx took) but an effective one to a rather strange, but effective, production. Caesar's battle-scarred veterans, as I recall, pranced onto stage wearing mini-togas and twirling hula hoops. Well, it brought the house down, and Sir John went on record saying that Robin Phillips had taught him a lot, which is some compliment.

Sir John spent his spare time at Chichester writing a book about actors and actresses he had known, called *Distinguished Company*. All those written about, unlike those hauled over the coals in some people's reminiscences, were dead.

'I think writing about one's contemporaries invidious,' he said, 'and in very bad taste. It causes trouble and disagreeableness.'

Some of her drawings, Zsuzsi Roboz says, had to be done pretty quickly. Sir John managed an hour and a half, and very obligingly put on his toga and his laurel wreath. So there he is as Caesar.

Eileen Atkins

THE COCKTAIL PARTY 1968. VIVAT! VIVAT! REGINA 1970

Miss Atkins was once employed as a cinema usherette, had a stroke of luck and was fired. 'I wasn't very good at it, which is why I was sacked. I used to sit in the stalls in a ghastly maroon uniform and dream that one day I would be a success like the stars on the screen.'

Well, she made it, via *Sister George*, in a taxing part which won her the *Evening Standard* Best Actress Award in 1965, ten years after handing in her torch.

Miss Atkins had ambitions once to be a playwright and got down to it at Stratford. 'It had everything, incest, lesbians, murder and rape. Then I read it through and found it lasted only 19 minutes. From then on I decided to stick to acting.' Seems a pity the theatre lost all that imagination.

Vivat! Vivat! Regina! was a huge success for her (and everyone else) at Chichester in 1970. Her Elizabeth, opposite Sarah Miles' Mary, was a wonder to behold. The play went to the West End and New York, not without slight complaint from Miss Atkins.

'I enjoy the part enormously, but it does make life a bit strange. It's very tiring—it sounds trivial, but there's never time to sit down during the performance, as even when Sarah Miles and I are offstage, we're changing our dresses and wigs.'

When she finished playing Elizabeth she said she'd lost a stone, what with the non-stop activity and the weight of her costume. She said thanks graciously to Robert Bolt for writing the part, the greatest interpretation of the lady, she thought, ever written. 'You cannot give a good performance unless you have a good role.'

Nevertheless, she was happiest in *The Cocktail Party* with Alec Guinness. Why? 'Simply because it was so difficult.'

Zsuzsi on Atkins: 'This is the expression she has that John Gielgud calls "catching flies".'

Roy Dotrice

'I have spent my life,' says Roy Dotrice, 'hiding behind face fungus and warts and false noses and wigs.' His Peer Gynt had none of these decorations. The Scandinavian dreamer's ageing process, therefore, had to be a matter of acting artifice. His prowess at playing old men dates from long practice at Stratford-on-Avon, where he found exaggerating two or three line parts a useful way of getting noticed and progressing from spear-carrier to star.

'I was playing such small parts I found that if I doddered a bit it made more impression on the company. This is where the character thing and the old man thing started creeping in. If I'd played them straight it wouldn't have created much impression.'

Mr Dotrice made it into the Guinness Book of Records with his impersonation of John Aubrey in *Brief Lives*, for playing more one-man performances than anyone else. Playing John Aubrey or any other old man, he says he likes to present as sympathetic a performance as possible, if only to persuade some of the audience to behave better towards any old people they happen to have around the house. He spent the intervals of *Brief Lives*, for instance, pretending to be dozing in his chair.

'I spent the time deciding how to do the second half. Parts of the play were interchangeable, and if the piss and fart bits did not go down too well in the first half, I rather played them down in the second and put in other things.'

Mr Dotrice began his career in a German prison camp during the war, getting roped in to play a chorus girl in pantomime because he hadn't started shaving yet. After the war he went back to his native Channel Islands and formed a company of his own, which was killed off in the 'fifties by television. After that—rep., spear-carrying, success, Aubrey, and more success.

His performance in *Peer Gynt* was highly praised for its technical accomplishment. Christopher Fry (who lives nearby) adapted Ibsen, and Sean Kenny designed the set.

Jeremy Brett

Midway through the season, Hollywood beckoned imperiously and Jeremy Brett went off to play Freddy in *My Fair Lady*. Laurence Olivier was generous, and let Mr Brett go.

The Arden play, says Mr Brett, was a fine piece of work. 'It was a good, serious, profound play, and it kept the customers away in droves, while Joanie [Plowright] in *St Joan* packed them in.'

He was Dunois 'I was staying with Bob Stephens in Winchester so I seem to remember spending most of my time driving back and forth.'

Mr Brett performed a signal service for his friend Mr Stephens, when it came to the production of this book. Mr Stephens had trouble sitting still while he was drawn, so Mr Brett took out his guitar and sang folk songs for the duration.

'I don't mind sitting still. I'm used to it. I have a brother who's a painter, but some people find it tedious to sit still for two minutes. I think I sang every song I could remember. At least it kept him quiet.'

Some of the folk songs were South American, gleaned during a six-month wandering of the continent during which the public heard nothing of Mr Brett. 'The public never noticed. I was told I was mad to go away, I'd never work again. The day I came back I got *Voyage Round My Father* and spent the evening drinking with John Mortimer.'

Mr Brett was born Huggins, the son of an Army general who sent him to Eton. General Huggins objecting to a good Army name being paraded through the theatre, Jeremy Brett Huggins became plain Brett, and hasn't done too badly.

Sarah Miles

During the run of the play, Miss Miles, admits, she ran home after one more exhausting performance and thumped her sleeping husband on the head. 'Why did you write this impossible play?'

Robert Bolt and Sarah Miles had spent the previous year and a half in Dingle, County Kerry, making *Ryan's Daughter*. Dingle at the time had 1,000 residents and 47 pubs and drove Robert Mitchum close to madness, but not Bolt. While he was there he wrote the final draft of *Vivat!* which was destined to have its first performance at Chichester before going on to London and New York.

I recall the two of them on the first night. It was difficult to tell which of them was under the greater strain. Mr Bolt, before the performance, was in that pleasant oasis, the hospitality room across the lawn from the theatre. He jumped, mistaking the doctor who had come to administer vitamin therapy for yet another interviewer with a tape recorder in his black bag. 'I didn't sleep last night. I shall sleep like a log tonight. I spent a year and a half writing this play. Everything's mortgaged to the hilt.'

Afterwards he was immensely relieved, as he had every right to be. Miss Miles looked as tired as she had right to be. She said she lost two stone in the run.

'I was desperate,' she said, 'to play the part, desperate to prove I was worthy of the brilliant man who wrote it. When you hear the mumble of voices out there and feel the great mass out there, waiting . . . I knew I had to prove, "I am worthy of this part, even though my husband wrote it, and come hell or high water, I'm going to prove it." '

The Queen thought she did, and cried to prove it, when Miss Miles' poor Mary, Queen of Scots is locked up in a dungeon.

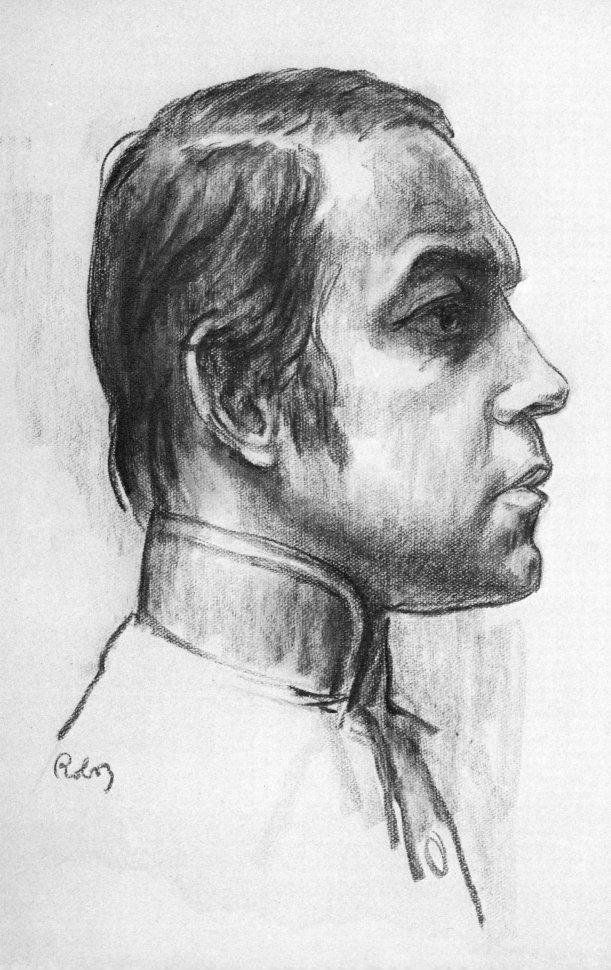

John Standing

Sir John Clements, according to John Standing, answers to the name of Fred, or Freddy. At least he does when addressed by John Standing, who is his step-son. The tag came in useful when Sir John Gielgud was at Chichester. There being two Sir Johns present, a confusing state of affairs, Sir J. Clements allowed that he might be known, for the time being, as Sir Fred. Fred was the name his step-sons called him by when children, preferring it to Step-Father.

John Standing is also Sir John (Leon, Bart.) but we will skip that. His mother is Kay Hammond. Zsuzsi Roboz says she kept seeing his mother in his face when she was drawing him. A resemblance like that could not be a bad thing in the theatre. It is said that when he played his first big part on the stage, an unmarried, orphaned actor (resting at the time, no doubt) was heard to grumble, 'I always said you had to have relations in this business.'

He began spear-carrying at Stratford, which does not require much influence. He has a son, Alexander, whom he says he hopes will not enter the family trade. 'Better,' he says, 'a rich businessman who'll help me through my dotage. I wouldn't have been an actor only I was too stupid to do anything else except paint, and I couldn't do that well enough.'

John Standing went to art school, gave it up, decided on acting, was told by Sir Fred that he was on his own, and went into rep. at Birmingham, making the odd television commercial.

'I did the first blue commercial. My trousers split as they filmed the scene.' He danced in pantomime. There were pretty ladies in the chorus, he explained.

His comic touch is light and fine, perhaps inherited. He is, or has been, frequently compared to the likes of young Rex Harrison or young David Niven. Characteristic modesty again: 'There's still *old* David Niven. He's marvellous.'

Dame Edith Evans

Dame Edith's appearance in this Anouilh play was unhappily short—she was forced to give up the part on medical advice after only a week's performance, but it was a performance, like all of hers, which made a great impact. She played an elderly actress lashing out at those around her with a fine sarcasm, fed the sort of lines that actresses delight in even if it gets them called actressy.

She began in the theatre at the age of 24 after getting fed up with millinery. James Agate called her 'this superb creature' and George Moore wrote her fan letters. 'You take acting as a sculptor takes marble,' he said.

Dame Edith herself was a little less reverent about the theatre. 'I'd like to have been a tap-dancer to tell you the truth,' she said. 'It used to drive me crackers.'

Bryan Forbes did a marvellous television film of her last year. 'I never feel like a great actress,' she told him, 'never. All I've ever done is never tell a lie on stage. They've had their money's worth out of me. They've had honesty and they were grateful. I've never tricked them, you see, I've never tricked an audience in my life. If I can't do it truthfully then I don't do it at all, because Shaw said to me once: "You're not worth ten pounds a week in a mechanical play because the minute you come you see all the works." He was right. I have to have the truth. I'm mad about the truth.'

(Dear me, one thinks of all those *other* actresses.)

During her brief stay at Chichester the theatre staff were naturally concerned to put as little strain on her as possible.

'Dame Edith,' said the photographer who had been snapping her for an hour, 'I do hope you aren't tired?'

'Dear boy,' she said. 'I've been tired for years and when I'm dying, I'll let you know.'

Anna Calder-Marshall

Anna Calder-Marshall, as a certain reviewer (myself) once said in the London *Evening Standard*, never does anything wrong. She did Cleopatra very well, positively bouncing round the stage, a spectacle which ought to have shamed any actress over the age of twenty out of the idea of trying the part herself, at least as Shaw wrote it. He did emphazize that *his* Queen was no fading vamp, but kittenish and fifteen, and full of the cruelty and charm of kittens and fifteen-year-olds, but not every director takes the trouble to solicit Bernard Shaw's advice on the production of his own plays.

Robin Phillips had taken that trouble (though his Sphinx, with paws fashioned from playground slides, struck a few of the audience as decidedly unShavian). Miss Calder-Marshall, under his direction, gambolled and twittered and shrieked with girlish laughter, and growled with murderous adolescent fury, and did her level best to run rings round John Gielgud's ageing but still wily Caesar.

She was herself twenty-three at the time, and had delighted her admirers (and perhaps made some of them jealous) four months previously by marrying David Burke, whom she met when they were playing the *Wild Duck* at Edinburgh.

She was a little worried in the dressing room on the first night. 'Did they notice me tripping over my dress?' No one noticed her tripping over her dress. She was very enthusiastic about Sir John.

'He's been a dream to work with,' she said, 'and taught me about nouns. "Anna," he once said, "you don't like nouns, do you?" It was because I wasn't making them audible. But oh dear, I don't want it to sound as if he's finickety. He's not.'

A year later she came back to play Jennet in *The Lady's Not For Burning* and this time Robin Phillips gave her platform shoes which elevated her six inches beyond her normal diminutive self. And she didn't trip that time either.

A T Smith

Zsuzsi had little trouble getting Mr Smith to sit for her. She is, well—married to him.

Mr Smith (or Teddy, as he allows himself to be called) had formidable talents which the founders of the theatre decided to tap. Not least of these was a facility for making money appear from nowhere. He had also considerable experience in the theatre.

He ran the New Lindsay Theatre in Notting Hill Gate from 1948 to 1957 (when it was pulled down), presenting a new play every three weeks, some of which, thanks to the Lord Chamberlain, might not otherwise have seen the light of day, and giving employment to such hopefuls as Dirk Bogarde and Kenneth More. After the New Lindsay, Mr Smith owned a share in the Duke of York's and helped turn it into a serious theatre.

No doubt all of this was familiar to certain people in Chichester.

'I had to go down there on business, to a firm called Wingard who do seat-belts,' Mr Smith explains with characteristic precision. 'Jim Battersby was the owner of it. He told me Evershed-Martin was endeavouring to put up a theatre. Fine, I said, but what's Chichester got to do with me?'

After a little inveigling, Mr Smith had a lot to do with Chichester. Becoming enthusiastic himself, he became chairman of the London committee, whose principal business was raising money. Raising £100,000, he explained, is simple.

The Earl of Bessborough had a meeting at the House of Lords. The Bishop of Chichester and the Duke of Norfolk (both locals, as it happens) were enthusiastic. (One peer was not, preferring to build a swimming pool.) Mr Smith got busy organizing various fund-raising functions and knocking financial guarantees out of people.

There was a ball at Arundel Castle on 12 May, 1961, after Princess Alexandra laid the foundation stone, with 850 generous guests. There were other extravagant entertainments.

The bills were all paid, the money was raised, and the theatre was built. Teddy did his bit.

Tom Courtenay

Tom Courtenay, who has made a habit of collecting awards, has another distinction not generally recognized; he has had more rubbish written about him by female journalists than any other living actor.

Nancy Spain: 'Tom Courtenay is a dish. His face has that brooding bony sort of melancholy Hamlet had, that Adam Faith has, that dominates the imagination in the same way as a statue by Michelangelo of a god from the pagan world. His eyes are magic. They suddenly unfocus themselves and drift away into a masculine dream world where the girls long to follow but never can.'

Anne Sharpley: 'He looked like a small, skinny gnome gazing into a cauldron and holding onto the bones of his face as if they might fall apart into his glass of vodka.' 'The emotions he inspires in me are to cook him a good supper and check to see he's got a clean shirt.'

God help us and save us. Zsuzsi does not appear to have been similarly unhinged. 'He has a dramatic expression which doesn't waver, not even when he's listening to a football match. He really came alive when he talked about football.'

Mr Courtenay is a fan of Hull City, from whence he came. He retains the accent. His father was a docker. 'I'm really an aristocrat,' he informed a questioner in 1961, when asked about his antecedents. 'I've only cultivated this working class thing after being at RADA.'

RADA came after an unsuccessful struggle with *Beowulf* and Eng. Lit. at the University of London. Mr Courtenay was for a while in the shadow of Albert Finney, whose part he took over in *Billy Liar* on the way up. He says he does a good imitation of Mr Finney.

Chichester was a return to the stage after a run of successful films. 'I honestly don't like big budget filming. It's not got much to do with acting—more to do with horses and guns. I want to learn about the art of acting, made good from top to toe.'

Mr Courtenay played cricket while at the theatre, borrowing an oak tree for use in lieu of practice nets. The Theatre XI took on a team of journalists. The result is not recorded.

Doris Hare

'The minute I saw Chichester,' says Doris Hare, 'I bought a house.' Most settle for cottages in the surrounding countryside. Miss Hare has one in the town, a few minutes' walk from the theatre.

She has appeared in four plays—*Trelawny of the 'Wells', The Farmer's Wife, Heartbreak House*, and Peter Shaffer's *Black Comedy*, which requires the actors, for the best part of the play, to pretend they are moving around in darkness. Since it is thought necessary for *the audience* to see what is going on, they are not in fact in darkness.

'I remember rehearsing it. Difficult? It was awful. So John Dexter had us blindfolded. You think you know where you are and suddenly find yourself in the street . . .'

The audiences found it delicious. After the first night eager patrons beseiged the box office *at night*. *Heartbreak House* was an equal success, transferring to the Lyric.

'I absolutely worship John Clements,' admits Miss Hare. 'But he is a great giggler on the stage and so am I. I thought "as soon we both get on stage I'll collapse". It nearly happened. He began it and I just had to dig my fingernails in my hands and struggle.'

On the theatre: 'The first time I saw it, I thought, how are you going to get a laugh in this barn? But as soon as you get the pitch right, it works marvellously.'

Miss Hare began early in the theatre—wowing the Americans in the thirties. They thought she was the best thing to hit them since Beatrice Lillie. More recently, she achieved fame as the mother in *On The Buses*. The Yugoslavs, she says, run after her in the streets when she is on holiday, calling 'Momma!'

I saw her at Portsmouth in 1972, when a crowd of Chichester people turned up in a successful attempt to save the Theatre Royal from demolition. She dashed off a Charleston with Bernard Delfont. Why him? He trod the boards there in his youth.

Sir Michael Redgrave

UNCLE VANYA 1962, 1963

Nice story about the possible non-existence of Vanessa Redgrave, told by herself: 'My father was playing Laertes at the Old Vic when I was born. A few days before I was born my mother and Lilian Bayliss were watching the play from a box. My father was rather over-excited at the thought of the coming event and played the duel scene in rather a wild way with Laurence Olivier. His sword flew out of his hand and came spinning right towards the box where my mother was sitting. Lilian Bayliss flung herself in front of my mother crying, "Oh God, not the dear child!" '

Nothing much to do with Chichester, but a nice story anyway.

Sir Michael does not pronounce as much in public as his daughter (or his son, for that matter). The temperament is quite different. One of our best Hamlets (Old Vic, 1949–50) he appears to feel little compulsion to philosophise, at least publicly. Never mind. His family does quite well in that department.

Sir Michael acts. He was Uncle Vanya in 1962 and the production was revived in 1963, going as well to the National. 'Uncle Vanya,' said The Times, in the days when their critic was still oracular and anonymous, 'lifts the National Theatre at last to greatness.'

Acting as natural as breathing, they said. Quite right, no doubt. Michael Redgrave is an easy man to write about as an actor. One reaches for the superlatives. Not so easy to write about as a private person.

He is a man, however, to involve himself. His signature appears on letters with other illustrious ones. At the first Chichester season there was a threat to demolish a row of Georgian cottages opposite the theatre because they were unfit (as they say) for human habitation. Enter Sir Michael, and others, in their defence. Council, puzzled at unaccustomed backchat, says, pained, 'We think these people ought to stick to their acting.'

Some chance. The festival, from its beginning, has been much involved with the place it is in.

Laurence Harvey

ARMS AND THE MAN 1970

The late Mr Harvey suffered a slightly bizarre accident at Chichester. He fell off a bed during rehearsals for *The Alchemist* and broke a bone in his right knee, this the week before he was due to play Sergius, the humourless Bulgarian officer in Shaw's debunking of the arts of war. It ought to have kept him out, but did not. He joined the cast a little later than he ought to have and even managed to turn the disability to good account.

Bluntschli, who does the debunking, remarks before Sergius comes on, that soldiers tend to break their legs in cavalry charges as the horses bang into one another. Enter Harvey, stiff-legged and avoiding the furniture, according to the *Daily Telegraph* critic, in a manner absorbing and elegant.

Mr Harvey, announcing he was a tramp and a vagabond, moved into Chichester in an altogether grander style, taking over the entire top floor of a hotel in Bosham, that pleasant and pretty seaside village a few miles from the theatre. He had been out of the theatre for a while and chose Chichester as the way back there after several years of making himself extravagantly famous and more than reasonably well-heeled in the cinema.

'You don't go to Chichester for money,' he explained 'You go to learn, to improve your knowledge of your craft. It's an investment.'

Mr Harvey had been so long out of the theatre he was pleased to discover he could still memorize two scripts. 'At least,' he said, 'there was the gorgeous certainty that, good or bad, I shouldn't be wandering around the stage like an idiot child, with the book in my hand.'

Nothing of the sort. It was the beginning of his successful return to the theatre.

Sad story: when he took his knee to the doctor, now knowing the extent of the damage, he was asked if he was in *The Alchemist*.

'Yes,' said Harvey.

'Ah,' said the doctor. 'Do you know anybody who wants to buy my tickets?'

Geraldine McEwan

Some of the critics were distinctly nasty about *Armstrong's Last Goodnight*. One of them said the language had the texture of haggis, which will not have pleased Mr Arden, but the same gentleman said Geraldine McEwan brought a much-needed touch of elemental sex to the proceedings.

Susceptible creatures the critics always were to feminine charm. Never more so than to Miss McEwan, for whom they went ape when she first appeared in the West End at the age of eighteen, playing a jilted Irish servant. She swept the floor in theatres before she made it, and had no formal training, which is in contrast with her husband Hugh Crutwell, who is Principal of RADA.

She says she learnt her business on the stage, in an eighteen-month run opposite Leslie Phillips. 'I learned enough to get myself to Stratford, which was what I wanted. But if you have no formal training you have an awful lot to catch up later if you want to do classical stuff, and then you have to get rid of the bad habits you have developed.'

No bad habits are evident. Miss McEwan's first words on the stage were 'Yes, ma'am,' from whence she has proceeded to greater things.

She spent six years at the National Theatre. Disaster for the National, said the newspapers when she left. Her voice is famous. It appears to stretch through as many octaves as an opera singer's. She seems very well aware of it, sometimes beginning a phrase somewhere below the alto range and ending well above the soprano, with swoops in between.

I remember that from *Dear Love,* an otherwise tedious Barrett-Browning vehicle (except for Keith Michell's equally fine performance) at the Comedy. I was sent to review it. I was going to be nasty but thought otherwise.

As I remarked, Miss McEwan has been sweeping the floor with critics for some time.

John Neville

John Neville, a political animal ('I'm working class. My father was a motor mechanic but he paid to keep me at school as long as he could') got fed up with being the idol of the gods at the Old Vic in the 'fifties and turned his efforts to making the Nottingham Playhouse into the best provincial rep. in the country, an episode that ended unhappily with Neville resigning, subsequently putting his political instincts and actor's tongue to use by making rude noises about the stinginess of Labour governments, general unsuitability of provincial theatre boards to run hot-dog stands, and so on.

Other political episodes: is fined £1 in the company of Vanessa Redgrave and others for obstructing traffic in an effort to prevent the world being blown up; gets Claud Cockburn and John Wells (some team) to write a play for Nottingham celebrating (if that's the word) the 1964 General Election. More rude noises, about politicians, artistic *gauleiters*, West End managements.

'I would like all the West End theatres blown up. They are antiquated and uncomfortable mausoleums that do not attract the young and vibrant audience they should be playing to. The trouble is mainly that the people who own the buildings haven't had a good idea since the days of gas footlights.'

Take that, Bernard Delfont, Emile Littler, *et al.*

Mr Neville became an enthusiast for provincial life and provincial people. 'I love provincial life. I don't ever want to go back. If I ever do move again, it might be to Africa. That's exciting.' Wasn't Africa as it turned out. Mr Neville headed for Edmonton, Alberta, where the climate is slightly different.

Neville the footballer, asked if he would like to manage a team: 'Yes, at least I have one outstanding qualification. I know what it's like to be sacked.'

Neville's father, after seeing the first night of *Alfie*: 'Cor blimey, mate, you're reverting to type, aren't yer?'

His Macheath, in 1972, in my opinion, was one of the best things in the theatre for years. The West End, true to his opinion of it, did not transfer it. Boneheads.

Anthony Hopkins

I met Jonathan Miller on the train when he was going down to direct *The Shrew*, and I, with a lot of people from Chichester, was going to Portsmouth in a successful attempt to save a lovely old theatre from demolition.

How was Hopkins playing Petruchio? Like his sergeant-major, said Dr Miller, launching on an imitation of Hopkins' imitation, no doubt exaggerated, of his sergeant-major. Strangled voice: 'I want you lot to be'ave yourselves. I want you to do what I tell you. I need you to do what I tell you, because if you don't, I shall be 'orrible. I 'ave a personality problem, you see. (Pause) I'm a cunt.'

First night. Joan Plowright, in her dressing-room, pointed rue-fully to the scar of her recent throat operation and her strapped foot. 'Someone has it in for me.'

Was Petruchio really based, as seemed highly plausible from the performance, on the sergeant-major, or was that an invention of Dr Miller's?

'Bloody right,' said Mr Hopkins. 'I was looking for this charac-ter and it suddenly came to me that it was Regimental Sergeant-Major Hackett of the Royal Artillery. I'm indebted to my sergeant-major. He's in New Zealand now. If I knew his number I'd ring him up and thank him.'

Mr Hopkins, like Sergeant-Major Hackett, is forthright in the pursuit of his profession, and inclined to be rude about members of the same. 'I want to become known all over the world. I am a vain man. I am also a good actor. Well, shall we say, a competent actor who is still learning.'

Hopkins joined a rep. company once, and got fired for taking part in a brawl. One of the officials, he claims, told him he had an odd-looking face and might have a flair for acting. He went to drama school and found he had.

Roboz

Sarah Badel

THE CLANDESTINE MARRIAGE 1966. THE FIGHTING
COCK 1966. THE CHERRY ORCHARD 1966
HEARTBREAK HOUSE 1967. AN ITALIAN STRAW HAT 1967
PEER GYNT 1970. ARMS AND THE MAN 1970

Miss Badel is Alan Badel's daughter and remarks on it, 'People are always surprised to learn that my father has a daughter as old as I am. My parents met at drama school and married when they were both eighteen.'

Miss Badel looked *so* ancient when she appeared in David Garrick's antique comedy (she was twenty-three at the time) everyone fell over themselves finding synonyms for stunning. A girl of remarkable loveliness, and possessing her own hair, said Londoner's Diary in the *Evening Standard*, which is usually restrained about these things.

None of her family turned up for the first night, for good reasons. 'My father's in *Man and Superman* and the others couldn't come for some reason for another. They never encouraged me or discouraged me from going into the theatre. They just let me do as I liked.'

That out of the way, it can be remarked that the Badels, particularly Sarah, have done well by Shaw, as has Chichester. Miss Badel played the noble Raina (the one that gets upset about keeping chocolates instead of bullets in one's bandolier) in *Arms and the Man* and Ellie Dunn in *Heartbreak House* and, also at Chichester, Solveig in Ibsen's *Peer Gynt*.

She has a cottage in remoter Sussex, which seems to be a habit with Chichester actors, and bought herself, for £200, an armour-plated ex-Army four-wheel drive vehicle to get there. 'It's ideal for the deep rutted track,' she remarked, 'and marvellous for going over ploughed fields and plunging through woods. It's very heavy on the wheel and it took a bit of courage to learn how to handle it. I use it for driving cross-country down to the nearest village to a very nice pub.'

So now you know it is not hallucination if you see a thirsty blonde driving an armoured car past the theatre.

Richard Chamberlain

Mr Chamberlain, as is universally known, got fed up playing a certain part on the box and decided to go straight, by entering the theatre. Where else but England?

His stage debut was as Hamlet, on the theory of diving in at the deep end. Caution, however, dictated that he made the plunge in Birmingham, believing, erroneously, that the critics, who are not normally crazy about trips to Birmingham, would have the grace to stay in London. Not so. They turned up in force, knives sharpened, but went to the telephones afterwards to report the fact that Mr Chamberlain could *act*. If he had not been acting with conspicuous brilliance before, perhaps it was merely that no one had asked him to.

He stayed with us, like many Americans of taste and culture. Mr Chamberlain's taste and culture, and exquisite manners, are now well known in the theatre. Sometimes he loses his temper with himself and says things like 'heck', but not often.

Mr Chamberlain played Mendip at Chichester, a character who is eager to be hanged but deprived of the pleasure by Anna Calder-Marshall, who, being a sensible young woman, does not want to be burned as a witch. The play, he said, was a tight-rope between comedy and fantasy. His English accent was by then impeccable.

'I met an American director, quite well known. He asked me if I thought I could play an American for him.'

'Richard was jumping up and down and saying "We've done it, we've done it,"' said his leading lady in the dressing room afterwards. (She could not jump up and down herself at the time because she was wearing shoes which elevated her six inches beyond her usual not-very-towering self.)

Christopher Fry came backstage too and thanked and congratulated everyone.

Sir John Clements

Sir John posed as Sir Anthony Absolute. Zsuzsi was admiring. 'A very difficult expression, but he kept it for long bouts.'

Dedication appears to come easier to him than to lesser mortals. In the days when he ran the Intimate Theatre in North London he produced 250 plays in five years and played the lead some thirty times a year. In 1951 he put on and starred in the whole of Shaw's epic *Man and Superman* which, including the Hell scene, runs for five and a half hours, which may be why the Hell scene is included once every twenty years or so.

Chichester must have seemed restful by comparison. Sir John took over as director in 1966 after Laurence Olivier quit, pleading the impossiblity of running both it and the National.

'In the old theatre,' Sir John then, 'the actor-managers once dominated—then they dried up, and there was nobody but Olivier, myself and Rix. This provincial thing is a new form of it. The wishes and ambitions once inherent are still present, but there were difficulties in realising them because of the economics of it. But with the changing provincial pattern, the actor-manager is coming forward again in a modern form.'

Sir John reigned for seven years and left the festival in much better financial shape than he found it, directing and acting in many plays himself.

His second year was not without its *longeurs*. There was the '*affaire* Kaye', and Hazel Penwarden, the leading lady in *An Italian Straw Hat,* retiring with an injured foot four days before the opening.

'There are times when, like the captain of a ship going through a typhoon,' he said, 'I would like to abandon ship, to duck my head and let it all go by. Even so, I cannot honestly say that I ever wish I had not entered the directorial field. Like most things, it has its problems, but I have been acting and working on the other side since 1935 and I am glad it is so.'

Albert Finney

Mr Finney was hanged at the end, a ritual many critics would like to see performed on many actors in many plays, if not Mr Finney and not this play. It was a realistic business and drew appropriate gasps from the audience, but he was able to bound back for thunderous curtain calls, thanks to a thin, invisible wire preserving him from strangulation. *Not* Mr Finney's last goodnight.

The Arden play went on to the Old Vic, and he was hanged in different circumstances, this time under a proscenium arch. The part offered certain challenges, chief among them being the need to speak in a sixteenth-century Scottish lowland dialect, *and* with a pronounced speech impediment. Heroism of more than one sort was obviously called for.

There was slight hardship too, that season. Albert Finney does not much care for possessions, but had come into the possession of a Phantom V Rolls-Royce. He doesn't like driving and his chauffeur had gone on holidays, so there were eight-mile taxi rides for the duration.

Mr Finney has a sense of humour.

'What's wrong with your hand?' he was asked by a reporter.

'I hit a journalist,' he said, smiling.

He got bitten by the theatre acting in a nativity play in Salford at the age of ten, demonstrated considerable talents imitating dogs, sheep and Al Jolson, got one O-Level out of six (geography) and a scholarship to RADA. He turned up with a thick Salford accent and a crew cut because the man who won Wimbledon that year had a crew cut.

He likes taking time off for travel in between triumphs, which are frequent. He is married to Anouk Aimée. He does not like talking about himself. 'What's the point?'

He has a social conscience. When he directed Brien Friel's play about death and politics in Londonderry, he said: 'When I first read Brian's play I wondered whether I should be directing plays or building houses for the underprivileged in Londonderry?' Directing plays.

Dame Sybil Thorndike

Dame Sybil played the Nurse Marina in this first season, amusing everyone inordinately with stories of the great when not so great, and obviously delighted with the new theatre, as was her husband, Sir Lewis Casson.

'We are both so thrilled about this new theatre,' she said. 'The joy—the joy of the open stage—and working with Larry again. We have known him since he was a child. His father and mine were both parsons in Pimlico. One day father Olivier asked Lewis and I to go and see his ten-year-old son playing Brutus in a church play. And, my dear, Larry was superb.

'There he was, striding the stage all done up in his white toga with his fierce little face staring above it . . . We saw him play Sir Toby Belch when he was twelve, and then, when he was thirteen, we saw him play Katharine in *The Taming of the Shrew*, and what a shrew that was. I have never seen better.'

She remembered another gentleman not unconnected with Chichester. 'I remember years ago when I was trying to teach Greek tragedy. I had thirty pupils and they all seemed so dull, all except one little lad in the back row. I was going mad. I rose up in my wrath and said, "You, boy, are the only one with any spark. What is your name?" '

'He stood looking at me, his pale little face quivering, and said, "John Gielgud".'

Dame Sybil was eighty in *Uncle Vanya*, and is now past ninety. I remember that birthday party quite well. There were also present Dames Agatha Christie, Edith Evans and Peggy Ashcroft. 'All me old pals,' said Dame Sybil loudly, 'it's a beautiful party,' and blew out the small forest of candles with a couple of gulps, before attacking the cake with a huge bread knife. 'Is this a dagger I see before me? Ah, gottim in the guts!' Cake becomes cadaver.

Zsuzsi says she saw Dame Sybil's lips moving quietly while she was being drawn and asked if she wanted anything. 'Just rehearsing, dear,' she said.

Keith Baxter

THE COUNTRY WIFE 1969. ANTONY AND CLEOPATRA 1969
TONIGHT WE IMPROVISE 1974

It was Mr Baxter's original ambition to be Archbishop of Canterbury, but for histrionic rather than ecclesiastic reasons: 'I used to sing in the church choir in Wales and each time the Bishop came to the church he wore the best frock and he sat in a beautiful chair, beautifully lit, and there were trumpets playing. I thought, if that is what the Bishop gets, imagine what the Archbishop of Canterbury must get.'

No doubt we have had the odd Bishop who has joined the Church for precisely that reason, but it seems a good thing that Mr Baxter was not lost to us that way, however splendid it might be to hear him preach a sermon.

Mr Baxter is, of course, Welsh, like half the acting profession. I do not know why the Welsh produce so many actors, but they do, and nobody's complaining. Mr Baxter went to RADA on a scholarship. Regional accents were not yet fashionable, not even Welsh ones.

'Somebody,' says Mr Baxter, 'said I sounded like my mother dug coal with her fingertips.' RADA erased the Baxter lilt.

His role at Chichester was Octavius, for which he was widely praised, even by my friend Milton Shulman, who does not praise lightly. Other parts with which he made a hit were Henry V in Orson Welles' *Chimes At Midnight*, and the wily young man in *Sleuth*. The Americans were so pleased with that one they made him the centre of New York's social life.

The ultimate accolade: *Cosmopolitan* invited him to take his clothes off for the benefit of their randy readership. He declined.

Margaret Leighton

'Miss Leighton,' said someone, 'never plays anyone vulgar.' True, unless you count Cleopatra, whom she played opposite Sir John Clements. Miss Leighton was not born to play anyone vulgar. Who will not treasure her line in *Lady Caroline Lamb*, informed that Lady Caroline has managed a theatrical death? 'Wouldn't she!'

'I think that if you have ever been or even half been a classical actress,' she said, apropos Chichester, 'not to go on and do Cleopatra really seems a bit feeble.'

Ten years had passed since Miss Leighton had last played Shakespeare, in *Much Ado About Nothing* with John Gielgud. Cleopatra she found more strenuous. Her characteristically candid explanation: 'You need more breath and I defy you to find a Shakespeare play that hasn't got a million steps or staircases in it. I have rather bad legs so it is hard for me to trail around. It was a great surprise to be so well received in the part—well, some of the Sundays said I wasn't sexy enough, but you can't suddenly act sexy. If you're not, you're not.'

Miss Leighton appears to have been captivated by Chichester. She and her husband, Michael Wilding, bought a house at the end of a lane at Birdham, two miles away, in time for her appearance in *Reunion in Vienna*. They cultivate strawberries.

Her comment on acting, which, it is generally agreed, she does rather well: 'The extent of my ambition is still not to get it wrong.'

And on the open stage at Chichester: 'I think you can't cheat as much. I don't think actors' backs are all that boring if they are doing it properly.'

Robert Stephens

SAINT JOAN 1963. THE WORKHOUSE DONKEY 1963
THE ROYAL HUNT OF THE SUN 1964. ARMSTRONG'S
LAST GOODNIGHT 1965. THE SEAGULL 1973

Robert Stephens, who does not look as if he needs the exercise, lifts weights. He once said his ambition was to be able to lift heavier weights than Laurence Olivier, who favours the same exercise, as well as the same theatres. Mr Stephens claims originally to have taken up weight-lifting to get rid of flat feet and a hollow chest, which seems surprising.

Anyway, robust actor that he is (among other qualities) he approves the solid virtues. 'All I recognize is bloody hard work. There's no time for outside activities if you do this work properly.'

Mr Stephens has been known to drink a bottle of Guinness (it's good for you, which is why they drink so much of it in Camden Town). He is not as severe as his pronouncements on the craft of acting might make him appear. (Stephens again: 'Hard work is good for you.' I hope aspiring stars are taking notice of this.)

He is versatile. 'All you can do is extend your range, see how far you can stretch before you snap. It's no good going on stage and saying, "Here I am, folks, look at me". As far as possible an actor should be unrecognisable as himself every time he appears.'

Evidence of versatility: he played the wooden-faced Atahualpa in *The Royal Hunt of the Sun* at Chichester in 1964 and the peevish Dauphin in *St Joan* the year before. 'John Dexter called up and said, "Listen, John Neville's just dropped out of *St Joan*, so would you like to include the Dauphin in the parts you'll be playing?" That clinched it. I was sure nobody else would ever cast me as the Dauphin.'

Mr Stephens makes a habit of knowing an *entire* play, not merely his own part in it, a suggestion he welcomed from Olivier but one I think most actors, being not so dedicated, would regard as a scandalous imposition.

Maggie Smith

It wasn't a bad part for an actress. Miss Smith was playing Desdemona opposite Laurence Olivier. 'She's marvellous,' said (the then) Sir Laurence.

Miss Smith, who was fond of describing herself as 'a pinhead who's all eyes and teeth,' was not awestruck. She turned it down to begin with. Her friends said she was mad. ('You can't *not* play Desdemona when Larry's doing Othello.') Returning from a holiday in Majorca, she revealed Sir Laurence had been on the same island. 'We met once. I can see him every day at home if I like. You don't want to meet people you work with on holiday, do you?'

Sir Laurence, while playing Othello (which went also, naturally, to the National) instructed Miss Smith in her vowels, which he thought imperfect. Miss Smith meets him in dressing room, blacking up. 'How now, brown cow?' she enunciates exquisitely.

'Better,' says Olivier, 'Much better.'

Miss Smith got into the theatre quite by accident, none of her family or friends being that way inclined. She claims never to have seen a play until well into her teens, then became a student ASM at the Oxford Playhouse for 15s 6d a week.

'I stood in the wings for five years, then I got a small part in a revue. I remember seeing my name, Margaret Smith, on the bills. It looked so awful I thought I'd change it. Some friends and I sat up all night thinking of glamorous stage names but they all sounded phoney. So I said to hell with it and asked the management to switch my name to Maggie.'

Since then a name rather well-known, if not immediately. Miss Smith, like many actresses, had cause to complain of being 'discovered' half a dozen times before becoming firmly fixed in the theatre's consciousness. Perhaps it was her versatility.

Miss Smith on herself, 1963: 'Even my best friends tell me I've got a bashed-in face. What do you think of my chances?'

Sir Noël Coward on Miss Smith: 'Divine!'

Miss Smith on why she prefers the theatre to the movies: 'You have very little dignity, dear. They shove the mike and the lines up through your knickers.'

Sir Laurence Olivier

Lord Olivier as art critic: 'He told me his nose was rude enough already,' said Zsuzsi, 'and now it was *very* rude, so I did another.' If he looks preoccupied it is because he was studying a report for the House of Lords, or so the artist reports.

The first night of *The Chances* was regarded as being of extraordinary importance for the theatre, not merely because it was the beginning of Chichester, with Sir Laurence as Director. It was not taken as coincidence that the Government had chosen the same day to announce (130-odd years late) that we were, after all, actually going to have a National Theatre *paid for* by the Government. There was little doubt in anyone's mind just who was going to be Director of the National.

3 July, 1962, was therefore taken to be the first public performance of at least the nucleus of the new National Theatre. So it turned out to be. A month later Olivier was named Director of the National, and took performances back and forth between both theatres for the next four years. (*Othello*, for instance, making the trip to London and then back again the following year.)

The performance was received very well, the acting and the production praised universally (even though Olivier was not in it, merely having directed). It being the occasion it was, some criticism was necessary (critics do get bawled out by editors for finding nothing wrong when the other lot did) so some grumbled about the choice of play.

The locals responded enthusiastically, except for some Men in the Street who said they'd rather have a swimming pool. They were given one. Actors like swimming too. Young Richard Olivier was christened in the Bishop of Chichester's private chapel.

The influence of the theatre on the National, through Lord Olivier, was profound. It is at least in part due to his experience at Chichester that the new National Theatre on the South Bank has an arena stage as well as a proscenium. It would be silly if it did not.

Simon Ward

Simon Ward managed three productions in 1968, the last reluctantly. His appearance in *The Tempest* seems to have had something to do with Sir John Clements' persuasiveness.

'I didn't want to do *The Tempest*,' confesses Mr Ward, 'but it was the very fact that I didn't want to do it, I think, that made me go down in the end. Ferdinand in *The Tempest* must be the most boring young man in Shakespeare. I studied it for O-Level *and* A-Level and I knew I was onto a bummer. Some unfortunate people have to do it *twice*. Not me.'

Mr Ward took a cottage and brought his family, which included at the time, he says, one daughter and one pregnant wife. (The result of the pregnancy was a second daughter. The two now compete in noise-making at the Ward house in Islington with a very rowdy dog.)

Ferdinand graced the cricket team, a prospect his creator initially found as petrifying as playing the role. 'It was the first time I'd played cricket in ten years, and I was always lousy at it. We were going to play the National and then the RSC but that all fell through, so we wound up playing the Military Police. I'd forgotten how terrified I was of cricket balls. Their fast bowler was six foot six with Brillo pads coming out of his chest. Out of sheer panic, I hit four off the first ball.'

Chichester won.

Comment on the theatre: 'Most terrifying job I've ever done. Instead of having a nice cosy little frame, you've got to give out for 360 degrees.'

Mr Ward wound up enthusiastic about that too.

Roboz

Beatrix Lehmann

Who's Who informs me that Miss Lehmann's hobbies are history and swimming, a fine mix. Her sister is Rosamond, the novelist, and her brother is John, the publisher and writer. She has published many short stories herself, and two novels. The first was written in Scottish dialect in a laundry-book pilfered from the kitchen.

Her parents objected, as so many do, to her going on the stage (why is acting so firmly classed by parents and careers masters with burglary and stunt flying?) but she persevered, supporting herself for four years by writing for a living (no mean feat, if I may say so).

The association with the theatre began in childhood, with sister Rosamond writing playlets and Beatrix appearing in them. RADA provided her with what expertise she could not pick up in the back garden, and her first work was touring the village halls of the south of England, precursors of Chichester and Stratford.

Miss Lehmann terrified London for many years, playing the parts of demented or evil ladies, a fashion which has now transferred from the theatre to the cinema with beneficial effect on the balance of payments, before settling down to the mastery of Shakespeare.

She played Aase, Peer Gynt's mother, in the adventurous production at Chichester in 1970, and a blowsy aristocrat the year later in *Reunion in Vienna*.

Miss Lehmann stayed in a cottage in Bosham while at Chichester, and was accompanied everywhere by her pet dog, which behaved itself.

Nigel Patrick

Archduke versus Psychoanalyst, and neither Johann Strauss nor Alban Berg to wrap the lines in musical plausibility. *Reunion in Vienna* had been a vehicle for the Lunts. Resurrected forty years after its composition, who better to impersonate an Archduke than Nigel Patrick? Bounder *sans pareil*, cad beyond compare, Mr Patrick made a splendid aristocrat nipping over the Austrian border for a sniff at his former mistress from the good old days before the revolution.

Mr Patrick has had much practice at playing cads and aristocrats (recall the *Great Waltz*?). Not quite as caddish as David Niven, was said to be the foreigners' opinion of him, but definitely more so than Rex Harrison, and just as English. (Foreign cads are not up to ours).

'Absolute so-and-sos,' he calls them. 'There's always a vague skeleton in the cupboard as far as I'm concerned, a bit of the four-letter man behind all of us.'

Mr Patrick is an enthusiast for the traditional theatre, making disparaging comments about 'those three gentlemen in urns down at the National Theatre.' There is room too for Brian Rix.

He has made a great many films, could have made a great many more, but prefers returning to the theatre, as the better sort of actor does. He joined the Army in September 1939 (as the better sort of person did) and emerged in 1946 a lieutenant-colonel, an experience he may have found good practice for his many officer parts. (There was that splendid performance in *The League of Gentlemen*.)

From lieutenant-colonel to spiv. After the war he says he played a run of them. 'Took me two years to shake off.'

There is room in the theatre, in his opinion, for all sorts of plays. 'All that matters is that the play should be good. It helps if its written in *real* English.'

Alastair Sim

Alastair Sim has a CBE; is an actor and director; is not spoken ill of by anybody; was born in Edinburgh on 9 October 1909 (which makes him a Libra, not that that is likely to matter to a man of his sense); was formerly Fulton Lecturer in Elocution at New College, Edinburgh; made his first appearance on the stage at the Savoy on 19 May, 1930, as the Messenger in *Othello*; and has two columns devoted to him in *Who's Who in the Theatre*, which is where I got most of this information.

Mr Sim prefers privacy to publicity, which is a source of irritation to journalists, but a preference which no doubt grants a great deal of peace and happiness to those actors able to indulge it. Mr Sim does not publicly pronounce on anything. The best-informed gossip columnist does not know what he eats for breakfast or how he votes, if he votes at all, in General Elections.

He did appear in a play called *Siege* in the West End in 1972, playing a Tory ex-Prime Minister, with Stanley Holloway, who is less reticent, as his butler. The director was Robert Kidd and the play was not in praise of the Conservative Party.

I was sent to ascertain Mr Sim's views on anything at all. He was very pleasant but said nothing which could appease the appetite of newspaper editors either for profundity or trivia.

What, I asked the director, did Mr Sim think of the left-wing slant of the play? Mr Kidd said he was agreeably surprised at Mr Sim's attitude. End of enlightenment.

Mr Sim played Lord Ogleby in *The Clandestine Marriage,* and came back to do the name part in *The Magistrate* in 1969, which was a great success and travelled to London, and played the gambling dean in *Dandy Dick* in 1973.

It is a matter of record that he has been very kind to his colleagues in the theatre. May he continue to evade the Press as long as he likes.

Keith Michell

It is news to no one that Keith Michell is now Artistic Director of Chichester and has had his first opportunity to mould a whole company with the twelfth season. But his acquaintance with the theatre goes back to its beginning. Sir Laurence Olivier, the first Director, cast him in the first two plays in 1962, as Ithocles 'a favourite, successful in battle,' in *The Broken Heart*, a blood and thunder epic by John Ford, and as Don John in a neglected Beaumont and Fletcher comedy, *The Chances*.

Sir Laurence described the plot as 'two Spanish blades going on a romantic journey in Italy and getting into some trouble', and all the critics reached for the word swashbuckling.

Christopher Fry, who is something of a local, wrote a prologue:

> *A theatre, speaking for the age*
> *We live in, has an ancient need;*
> *The link between audience and stage*
> *For which I come to intercede.*

The link was immediately established. Indeed the audiences seem to have been a little startled at the energy of it. Audiences in 1962 were not yet used to actors thundering up the aisles, but in time even the critics got used to it.

Sir Laurence gets the credit for discovering Keith Michell. He was born and educated in South Australia 200 miles from Adelaide in an area which was not overpopulated, and spent a solitary childhood drawing and painting. He still takes time to paint in between performances, but he gave it up as a career after winning a place at the Old Vic school.

He is now principally famous for his television portrayal of Henry VIII, and for his adherence to a macrobiotic diet. He says he loved Chichester from his first appearance there and always returned for the seasons.

Zsuzsi Roboz drew him as Abelard in *Heloise and Abelard*. His expression may have to do with the fact that the character he plays has just suffered castration, but Zsuzsi says he was suffering from a bad hip at the time.

'Abelard'

Roloz

Irene Worth

Miss Worth, for an actress who favours the avant-garde, has done herself proud in the classic parts. *Heartbreak House* is now by way of being *the* classic English play of this century (being written by an Irishman) and Hesione Hushabye a part to get your teeth into or else fail badly.

'No one,' said Ronald Bryden, 'has expressed Shaw's image of the Eternal Feminine more exactly.' Quite true, I thought, when I saw it transferred to the Lyric, though I do not think most women thank Shaw for his version of their eternity.

'I hate my face,' said Miss Worth then, complimented on her performance. 'I never primp, I hate looking in the mirror, I hate photographs. I think I have no talent. Why do I think that? Because no one's ever told me I have, I suppose. Oh, those notices don't count.'

She admits under pressure that she has had many rather splendid notices. 'I do think that I have been able to give truly modern interpretations of Shakespeare.' For which we are duly grateful.

Miss Worth went off with Peter Brook's troupe to explore new avenues of expression in Paris and Persia, in which place they invented a sort of new language, not precisely articulate, but having the virtue of being equally incomprehensible to unlingual Persians, English, Americans, French etc.

'When Peter asks you to do something you don't say no.'

'The experiment is really to free oneself from the inhibitions of the actor's craft. I still have many inhibitions. Acting for me should be as simple, natural and unmannered as possible. This is the goal in my life.'

Meanwhile, Miss Worth is a damn' good actress in the old, crafty, inhibited way.

Frank Finlay

SAINT JOAN 1963 . THE WORKHOUSE DONKEY 1963
THE DUTCH COURTESAN 1964 . OTHELLO 1964

Frank Finlay is a conscientious actor who likes to read himself into parts, Hitler and Casanova being the strangely assorted pair he recently found it necessary to study. Jeremy Brett recalls his spending most of his time at Chichester reading.

His Iago was a considerable success. It got him an Oscar nomination after being made into a film and he won the best actor award at the San Sebastian Film Festival, which wasn't bad considering who was playing the Moor.

'I remember going home delighted with something Olivier had said,' he recalls, 'and bursting to tell my family about it, but when I got in my daughter Cathy came up all excited and said, "Daddy, I'm top of the class," so I never did say anything about it.'

He began his career with the Bolton Amateur Little Theatre. 'I was a butcher for nine years from the age of fourteen, with an ambition to be a sanitary inspector, lording it over the abbatoirs. Where I come from, acting just isn't the thing you do for a living.'

Nevertheless he persevered, earning £1 a night for amusing the celebrants at local weddings with a stand-up comic act (part of which depended on poking fun at the Irish). He got a RADA scholarship aged twenty-seven, remembers feeling a little awkward because the other students were somewhat younger.

He arrived in London with wife, and child, and their belongings packed in a pram. 'We arrived at Euston. Taxis were out of the question and they wouldn't let the pram on the tube, so we pushed it to Waterloo. I can remember thinking about the Old Vic, but I never thought I would be one of the leading actors there.'

Mr Finlay has made more than thirty films. For the record, he was the first person to impersonate Jesus on the London stage, in Denis Potter's play.

He played the name part (a Labour councillor, not the lower form of life suggested by the title) in Arden's *The Workhouse Donkey*.

Millicent Martin

Like a Madonna in repose, said Zsuzsi of Miss Martin's features, which are very beautiful but have been more used to provoking laughter than piety. 'The moment her face moves, she becomes totally different. After a while, when people sit, they become themselves, because you can't keep up a pose. It's the other side that people know, but this is *her*.'

Miss Martin, in Wilder's comedy, had competition from a dinosaur, a mammoth and two drum-majorettes and was required to chat the audience up from the edge of the stage, none of which strained her comic talents.

'I prefer laughter to applause,' she has said. 'Clapping is some-something an audience *does*. Laughing is something they can't help doing.'

The part of Sabina was created in this country by Vivien Leigh and Miss Martin was asked rude questions at the time, by people who were used to seeing her on the box and thought she ought to be intimidated.

'If you're going to put yourself up as an Aunt Sally,' she said cheerfully, 'then you might as well make it a big one so everyone can hit it if they want to.'

Well, nobody did, and Miss Martin came back to Chichester in 1972 and did Polly Peachum in *The Beggar's Opera*. Now that was a great piece of fun. I wished, with many, I had been able to see it a few more times, and it reminded Milton Shulman that the play had lifted more actresses than any other to the peerage.

I thought when he made the remark, surely Miss Martin deserved a peerage in her own right. We haven't given one to an actress yet.

Topol

THE CAUCASIAN CHALK CIRCLE 1969 · R LOVES J 1973

This was Topol's first appearance in England in a 'serious' play after we had come to know him from the strenuous *schmaltz* of *Fiddler on the Roof*. There was some anxiety that he might not make it. His performance as Tevye in 1967 had been interrupted for a while by the more important business of the war his country was fighting. (Topol came back when it was over, which was more than could be said for Mr Danny Kaye, who contracted to appear at Chichester that same year, and pulled out ten days before production, pleading the necessity of entertaining Israeli troops. But let that pass.)

In 1969 there occurred one of the intermittent Middle Eastern crises. U Thant, in his wisdom, declared a state of war existed. As it happened, it did not, but there were fears that Sergeant-Major Topol would be unavailable to adorn Brecht.

Topol kept his cool and shaved his head for the part of Azdak, a drunken clerk who becomes a judge, resembling, after the shearing, no one so much as Telly Savalas. He thought it was worth it.

'I wanted to do it as it deals with confusion,' he said, reasonably enough, considering the state of the world, 'and the world is very confused at the moment. The play offers no answers but it does ask the right questions.'

Topol admits to a considerable sympathy for Brecht and reveals a slightly unexpected ambition. He wants to play the name part in *Mother Courage*: 'I feel she is really a man. Her chemistry is that of a man. She comes through with all the strength of a man. With Brecht's idea of alienation, even if the audience did look at it as a man dressed up as a woman, it could be done, perhaps. I don't know.'

A curious and charming idea. At any rate, his next performance at Chichester was not to be Mother Courage (or Mistress Quickly either) but the President of Concordia in Ustinov's *R Loves J*.

Topol has the pleasant habit of accumulating Israelis wherever he goes. 'I got half the Israeli Army here,' he said in his dressing room on the first night of Brecht. True, and one of them was Daliah Lavi.

80

Celia Johnson

Miss Johnson, it's been said, came to grips enthusiastically with middle age long before it was necessary, particularly in so beautiful a woman. Put her in a crumpled cardigan and old tweed skirt and give her a brush to sweep the odd bit of coal dust into the grate, and you get—a faded English rose.

Madame Ranyevskaya is not quite the same thing, if something in the same line, certainly not an easy part to play on the open stage. There were no complaints.

Miss Johnson began, after RADA, as Sarah in *Major Barbara,* played Olga in *Three Sisters* during the Festival of Britain and *St Joan* at the Old Vic before that, so not all her parts have been maternal.

She has played the maternal role most effectively in her private life. Her husband was Peter Fleming, the author and explorer. They had three children. She was, say her friends, the placid centre of a happy family. It was not to be guessed *there* that she had a life of her own.

Noël Coward and Terence Rattigan knew otherwise, and sought to have her in their plays.

In *Brief Encounter*, she created the best part of the greatest British weepie of all time.

And a critic once devoted three-quarters of his review to her eyes.

Leslie Evershed-Martin

Mr Evershed-Martin has the proud title, Founder of the Theatre. It was entirely his own idea.

On 4 January, 1959, Mr Evershed-Martin happened to be watching television. Tyrone Guthrie appeared on the *Monitor* programme, of blessed memory, and explained to Huw Weldon how he had brought the theatre to Stratford, Ontario, a town previously distinguished for nothing at all, thereby immeasurably improving the quality of the lives of its citizens.

Chichester was, of course, a town already distinguished in many ways. But Mr Evershed-Martin, who is a highly civic man (indeed an ex-Mayor of the town) thought it would be a good idea to have a theatre to add to its glories. He went to Stratford (our own Stratford, that is) to discuss the business of getting one with Sir Tyrone, losing little time. (That was 12 March, as a matter of fact.)

Sir Tyrone was properly enthusiastic. It was due to his advice that the theatre was built to its splendid design, which is something like the one in Ontario.

It was built at a time when a more normal activity was to pull a theatre down. 'The country,' the Founder remarked, 'was suffering its most depressing shrinkage in terms of theatres and cinemas, and had our idea been less accurately tuned to a parallel public demand, then only in its infancy, the pessimists (and there were naturally quite a few) would have triumphed and the flame would have died.'

Well it didn't. 'To start a prairie fire,' says Mr Evershed-Martin, 'there must be a spark, and it must be nourished by a fair wind on the right quarter and a parched land nearby to burn.'

Mr Eversham-Martin was the spark, and we were the parched land that burnt.

Fenella Fielding

Miss Fielding is one of those actresses who calls people, with no great deal of discrimination, 'darling'. Not that they mind.

'Darling,' she said, surrounded by chaos after the first night of *The Beaux' Stratagem*, plastered in flowers, 'there were lots of things I did tonight I shouldn't have done, and maybe won't do again. After a while you get in a sweat, you know, and don't know *what's* going on. You won't get any sense out of me, darling.'

Tragedy. Miss Fielding occupied her spare time, between rehearsals, taking driving lessons. 'I can do all the gears,' she reported, 'and I can reverse, but I can't get around corners yet.' She flunked her test (surprised?) but being the lady she is, bought a white Triumph Herald to celebrate.

1967 was the summer Mr Kaye did not turn up (for explanation, see elsewhere). He was to have appeared opposite Miss Fielding in *The Servant of Two Masters*. 'I can't say that I am desperately heartbroken,' growled Miss Fielding, 'just very angry. I don't know whether his previous experience would have suited him for the role, but he would have found it a fantastic experience.'

Ha! Take that, Danny Kaye. Chichester put on *An Italian Straw Hat* instead, graced by Miss Fielding. The public was so savagely disappointed at Mr Kaye's absence that twenty-two of the customers booked for thirty performances cancelled.

'There are such *physical* hazards, darling,' she said of the play. 'There are those stairs which I'm absolutely *bound* either to fall up or fall down.' No such thing happened.

Miss Fielding had given up a part in a Fellini film to appear. 'Everybody still says I'm wrong, but I simply know I'm not. You learn more at Chichester.'

Final tragedy. Miss Fielding was burgled of £60 worth of jewels, found her flat ransacked when she got back from the theatre. I suppose the burglars must have seen the play already. Bad critics, if so.

Fay Compton

THE BROKEN HEART 1962. UNCLE VANYA 1962 1963
THE WORKHOUSE DONKEY 1963

Miss Compton began her career in the Follies in the days when the male offspring of dukes and marquesses were still hanging around with bottles of champagne and invitations to dinner at Romanos, begging for the loan of a slipper to drink from.

'I got an audition for the Follies through my brother, Sir Compton Mackenzie,' she records, 'who was then working on a review for the Alhambra. I was a good mimic and pianist and could sing a little and the Follies needed a general understudy at £3 10s a week. I got the job.'

Miss Compton got the job after running away from a finishing school in Auteuil. She has been complimented, unsurprisingly, for her French accent. 'I learnt French at finishing school, and that school finished me, dear. It was *so* boring. I ran away when I was sixteen.'

There were decades of fame and a sad period of eclipse, when she could complain, in Coronation year, 1953, that no one had offered her any part in the theatrical celebrations of the time. Justice triumphed. Miss Compton got the plum part in a religious play by Christopher Hassall in Westminster Abbey, no less.

She was not above accusing the impresarios of ingratitude, but if they ignored her, television did not. ('Television? I loathe it. It frightens me even to watch it.')

The same with Shakespeare, apparently. After playing Ophelia: 'How do I like acting Shakespeare on steep steps and a rostrum? I don't like acting Shakespeare anywhere. It terrifies me.'

Never mind. Miss Compton, terrified or otherwise, has adorned many classics. And she always was a very witty comic actress.

(Some critic incautiously compared her to Sarah Siddons, one of her 'distant forebears.' 'How does he know?' she asked. 'Did he ever see Mrs. Siddons?')

Peter Ustinov

THE UNKNOWN SOLDIER AND HIS WIFE 1968
R LOVES J 1973

I don't know why Clementi, inventor of the pianoforte, traditional instrument of torture for small male children, should be buried at Westminster School, but Ustinov, who went there at the same time as the odious Ribbentrop's son, says he is. On one of our several meetings, Ustinov, whose conversation leads by devious processes towards situations which can be milked for comedy, mentioned that he had revisited the place. (Perhaps he had, and perhaps Clementi really is buried there.)

'I am pleased,' he said, 'to note that the custom of beating boys for stepping on Clementi's grave has died out. I still can't listen to his music without a shudder. I remember being on officer training manoeuvres with Ribbentrop's son, who habitually sneered. I was given a rattle to represent a machine gun. We were attacking Merchant Taylors' while unknown to us Lancing were attacking Marlborough across the same ground. Some of the boys never got home.'

Mr Ustinov, you may note, is all right as long as you keep feeding him lines, even *one* line, which normally is good enough for half an hour's flow of amusing, if one-sided conversation. Extricating oneself gracefully is another matter.

I recall the first night of *The Unknown Soldier and his Wife*, when I was sent backstage into the usual barrage of champagne, flowers and stentorian shouts of 'Darling!' to ask Ustinov the sort of idiot questions which are supposed to provide material for what the newspapers call an 'overnight piece'.

The train was leaving early, the only thing I can think of to say against Chichester (or British Rail, to be fair.)

'Thanks very much, Mr Ustinov,' I said, 'that's all I have to ask you.'

'What a pity,' said Ustinov. 'If you had more to ask I'm sure I would have been fascinating.' Collapse of audience, ignominious retreat of journalist. Never mind, he has been very civil on subsequent occasions and I would not want reporters in my dressing-room either.

The Unknown Soldier went on from Chichester, after an interval, and appeared for a long run in the West End, as plays from Chichester have a habit of doing.

Joan Plowright

Miss Plowright, who did not need one, had a certain *entrée* to Chichester. She was married to the boss. He chose this Jacobean comedy to inaugurate the theatre, and his wife played a creature 'panting to be ravaged' (Milton Shulman). She appeared also in *Uncle Vanya* the same season.

The Chances had not been aired since 1808, Lord Olivier having found the text by accident while browsing in the British Museum. It was a splendid opening and the theatre itself, almost, but not quite, stole most of the reviews.

Miss Plowright had been delivered of a child six months previously, but Chichester has the advantage that it does not take much time out of one's life. Later she took two years off to raise children and said, when she returned to the theatre, 'You find yourself getting terribly bossy. When we have people to dinner I practically find myself telling them to finish up their greens.'

Miss Roboz detected this trait, I suspect. 'I admire the way she deals with her life and her children and her career,' she said of Miss Plowright. More technically: 'One gets the impression of very high cheekbones. In fact this is not so. It is from the character she modelled into the stage image.'

Miss Plowright on being an actress and not being an actress: 'My job on stage is to act a character. I have no nervousness about that—but I just hate acting myself in public. It's worse than a first night.'

Treasured story, filched from *The Observer*, about Miss Plowright's antecedents. Her father contributed to the *Sheffield Telegraph*, where he was known as Plowright of Scunthorpe.

Plowright of Scunthorpe sends in scoop: 'Miss Joan Plowright, daughter of a Scunthorpe journalist, Mr W. E. Plowright, is to marry Sir Laurence Olivier, the actor. Ends'

Sheffield Telegraph, finding the story interesting, cables for further details. 'When asked for his reaction,' replies Plowright of Scunthorpe, 'Miss Plowright's father, Mr W. E. Plowright, said "No comment".'

Michael Aldridge

THE FIGHTING COCK 1966. MACBETH 1966
THE FARMER'S WIFE 1967. HEARTBREAK HOUSE 1967
AN ITALIAN STRAW HAT 1967. THE TEMPEST 1968
THE CAUCASIAN CHALK CIRCLE 1969
THE MAGISTRATE 1969. DEAR ANTOINE 1971
CAESAR AND CLEOPATRA 1971. REUNION IN VIENNA 1971
THE DOCTOR'S DILEMMA 1972. THE LADY'S NOT FOR
BURNING 1972. THE BEGGAR'S OPERA 1972

Michael Aldridge has difficulty remembering quite how many plays he has done at Chichester. There was *The Farmer's Wife, Heartbreak House, An Italian Straw Hat, The Cocktail Party, Antony and Cleopatra*—enough to be going on with. He recalls spring as being the time of the year when Sir John Clements would ring him up and enquire, as if he were not reasonably confident of the answer, what Mr Aldridge would be doing that summer.

His first appearance was in 1966. 'I'd been ill for months and doubted I could go on acting. I even thought of going to Bristol to direct students, rather madly thinking that might be easy. I turned down *Dr Who* and then was offered Chichester. It was marvellous, and I had started back again.'

Mr Aldridge demonstrated his enthusiasm by buying a house. 'I am not a city man. I can manage a town about the size of Chichester and I was lucky. I walked into a pub, a man heard me say I wanted a house and pressed a piece of paper into my hand. It said "keep this to yourself but I'm selling my house." '

The theatre also met with approval. 'It's the only theatre I've ever worked in where you meet everybody you're working with. Normally, if you're an actor, you go in a different hole in another street. In London you can be starring in a piece and go round to the box office and they don't know who you are, which is a little narking. In Chichester you even meet the girls from the restaurant because they use the loos backstage. You *even* meet the public, which at first is horrifying.

'And there is the ridiculous pleasure of working in a field, with a view.'

Heather Sears

Motherhood and Miss Sears' ambitions: 'I'm not getting so many of the virginal parts I've always played. I'm closer to my ambition of playing a real bitch.'

Her children, three of them, somewhat limited Miss Sears' appearances in the theatre and on film in the 'sixties. The ideal life, she said, would be to spend six months as Mum and six a star. 'I work in between having babies to save for the next one. I would hate to feel that my youngest child was going to be my last.'

Hmmm. Not fashionable sentiments. Miss Sears' returned to the stage in 1966 at Guildford playing a sixteen-year-old in something called *The Door*, which the *Evening News*, always splendidly literate, said was about 'a lovely girl, born into one of the richest families in the town, who has a dream.' Sounds great, but they spoilt it by calling her 'that bonny little actress'.

Miss Sears' (from Mile End, incidentally) role at Chichester was not bitchy, rather the opposite, a long-suffering lady called Grusha.

After Chichester, the West End, in *How The Other Half Loves,* which, as is history, ran and ran and ran and probably still is. She went also to the King's Head theatre pub in Islington, which deserves a plug when opportunity presents itself, being one of those places where it is possible to drink while watching accomplished actresses like Heather Sears.